The **POWER**

of your

Words

and

ACTIONS

Inspiring Stories I've Heard, Lived, and Like to Share

by

Wayne Soares

ISBN 978-0-9795444-0-8

For more information, visit www.SummerlandPublishing.com.

Printed in the U. S. A.

Library of Congress #2007929615

Dedication

This book is dedicated to the two greatest people
I have ever known: my grandfather, William "Blink" Soares,
and my grandmother, Jessie Soares, and also to the light of
my life—my daughter Jessie.

Testimonial

The Power of Your Words and Actions provides the reader with a summation of interesting, thoughtful and "feel-good" life examples that the author, Wayne Soares proudly shares with his audience during speaking engagements around the country. The truly neat thing about this publication is that those people impacted by his words will grow immensely through the power of print.

Wayne Soares is a professionals' professional in the art of drawing his audience to his level of sincerity and integrity and at the same time, being completely humble in his presentation. He has shared his thoughts and views with thousands of anxious listeners who, without a doubt, at the completion of his presentation, were highly motivated to do the right thing and to access their current values and ideals with respect to his great message.

I have been fortunate to hear Wayne Soares speak on many occasions and each time I came away with a new breath of fresh air to my thought process and outlook on life. Reading the *Power of Your Words and Actions* will provide you insight into the man and his enlightening perspective on life and the impact we have on the lives of others.

Martin E. Ryan, CMAA
Athletic Director, Kennebunk High School
Executive Director
Maine Interscholastic Athletic Administrators

Forward

by Rico Petrocelli

**(Former major league baseball player and member of the
Boston Red Sox Hall of Fame)**

When someone says to you, "This is the greatest person I ever met,"
we roll our eyes and think to ourselves, "C'mon who are you kidding?" I
agree with that statement but if there is one person I know who comes close,
it's Wayne Soares. He and I worked together on a radio Sports Talk Show in
Boston as co-hosts, and I have heard him speak many, many times at
Colleges, High Schools and to Business Groups. The response was
overwhelming. People loved his humor and real life stories. He can
empathize with people because he has gone through many of the same
experiences as the audience.

We've been friends for as many years as I can remember. I know
him as a compassionate, caring man. He especially loves Jessie, his
daughter, who he showers with love every day of the year. When Wayne
mentioned that he was writing this book I wondered if he would be able to
capture his great sense of humor and his passion to help others in the written
word. Now that I've read this book, there is no doubt that he has done just
that. His stories about his own experiences with his children and the wisdom
that he shows and the advice he gives comes from his own experiences and
of those close to him. I know you will enjoy this book and you will also take
away some incredible life lessons. We all want to do the right thing with
family, friends and people in general. This book will help you do it.

Life Has Special Times— How To Catch The Really Big Ones!

I would like to confess that I am a former workaholic. Yes, workaholic. I worked all the time when my two boys were five and seven years old. My daughter had not come along yet.

After watching a fishing show on television one winter afternoon, my two boys, Wesley and Spencer, had become fixated on having an afternoon of fishing with their Dad. That would be me, reluctant me, as you shall see.

I did my best to put them off, explaining that I had a great deal on my plate right now and this was an important part of my career. ESPN Radio had just hired me after I paid my dues in the local radio business—I had *big* plans for a wonderful career.

The boys' constant nagging about going fishing began to get me exasperated. It got to the point where I would come home and literally try to avoid them by going in the back way. I would slip into my office, my sanctuary from two wannabe fishermen, and there I would immerse myself in my all-important work.

When even this did not deter them from stalking me, I decided to confront them and try to reason with my young sons. I planned to sit them down in the living room after dinner one night and tell them why I work so hard. I had my strategic plan ready three days in advance, and was ready to give them all the reasons I had no time for them. I was fully prepared to play the "I'm Working Hard For *You*" card. That oughta' hold 'em!

But what really happened showed that I had underestimated their determination to drown some worms with me! I was really into it as I paced the floor telling the kids "I put in long hours and work all the time so that we can live in a nice house, go on vacations and so we can have a nice family car."

I was so full of myself as I explained that "You need to lay a foundation to build an empire and…"

My youngest son Spencer stopped me in my tracks. "Dad, that's great that you work hard for us, but *can we go fishing?*"

Shaking my head in frustration, I made my way to my office, leaving Spencer's question hanging in the air, unanswered.

I was so intent on becoming a broadcasting success that I would often demand that the boys "leave me alone and stop asking me about stupid fishing."

I now often speak about the power of our words and how they can affect people. But at that time, I myself was oblivious to the fact that I was using harmful words to fend off my boys' legitimate claims to their father's time. In my haste to become successful, I was actually forfeiting a true relationship with my kids. Friends, it's not worth the price.

Fortunately, common sense (and a dash of guilt) finally prevailed as I came up with the bright idea of getting each son a fishing rod for Christmas. They were happy, I was happy. They were delighted; I was delighted. They wanted to go fishing, I still did not want to fishing! I was too busy.

Getting the equipment only added fuel to their fire. Now they played every angle, constantly, to hook me into going fishing (puns intended). Finally, I succumbed. I will remember that day for as long as I have all of my marbles in my head. It was Sunday, July 17th, and I had been up since 6:30 a.m., typing away in my office—working, working, working.

At 7 a.m., I heard the dreaded knock at my office door. I looked up and it was my boys. They were greeted with "what do you guys want now?" instead of "good morning guys, how'ya doing?" I explained to the boys that I had a ton of work to complete and would probably be working all day until dinner.

When my kids want something from me they try to play me like a violin, laying on the charm every chance they get. "How's our favorite father today?" they asked cheerfully.

"I'm your *only* father. What do you want?"

"It's a nice warm day out," Spencer observed.

"A nice day to catch some fish," Wesley added with a mischievous smile.

In typical fashion, their old man wasn't to be swayed. "Guys, it's going to be over one hundred degrees today. There is no way that I'm leaving this office and my AC. I just have way too much work to do today."

Spencer, the youngest, took my day planner out from behind the door. The one thing I lived my whole life by was my schedule and my day planner.

"Where did you get that?" I asked.

"I snuck down last night when you were asleep in your office chair and took it," he said with a grin. "Hey dad, today is the 17th, right?" he inquired.

"Yeah, all day, now give that back to me." I snapped.

"But you have nothing on here for the 17th," he protested. "Absolutely nothing."

As I snatched the day planner from his hands I saw only a blank page for July 17th. Man, I thought to myself, I know I had *something* to do today.

Wes saw the chance and pounced on it. "Can we go fishing now?" he asked.

I stared ahead, feeling trapped for a second, then I countered with, "Why don't you two go outside and dig some worms for a few hours, then come back and we'll see."

'Score one for the old man,' I thought while mentally patting myself on the back.

Wes reached around the door and produced a red bucket, grinning all the while.

Dad: "What the heck......."

Wes: "Dad, we set our alarms for 5 a.m. this morning all by ourselves!"

Dad: "Lemme guess...."

Wes: "Dad, we've been digging for over two hours."

Dad: "And you have....?"

Wes: "Worms"

Dad" "Worms?"

Wes (excited): "In the bucket!"

Dad (dismayed): "In the bucket..."

Spencer: (bursting with excitement) "37 worms in the bucket, baby!!"

Dad (very bummed): *Oh boy!*"

I made the executive decision to spend "only one hour at the lake" and my boys stuck on me like Velcro meeting Velcro, screaming all the while about what a great Dad they had and how super I was. Little did I know how my next words would come back to haunt me later in the day.

"Guys, this is a waste of my time today. I don't even want to go, but we'll spend one hour at the lake because you're so spoiled. *One hour* and that's it."

The boys packed the car (so I thought) and we were on our way. They were buzzing in the back seat when a question from me brought dead silence.

"Did you two bring your rods?"

Back we went to get the new rods that had been left on the back steps of the house.

Arriving at the lake in temperature bordering 98 degrees, we made our way down to the edge of the lake. I warned them that I would not be going near the water as I had brand new sneakers on and didn't want to get them dirty.

"You guys can bait the hook and take any fish off your own hooks," I decreed as I grabbed a diet coke and a bag of chips, then retreated to the shade of a nearby tree. I planned a quick power nap of 15 minutes or so.

I awoke almost two hours later to find two poles in the water and no boys. My heart raced and I felt a knot in the pit of my stomach. I jumped to my feet and quickly looked around.

Relief came over me as I spotted my son Wes to my left, making castles in the sand. Looking right, I found Spencer hitting leaves on a tree and singing 'Old MacDonald Had A Farm' at the top of his lungs.

It took me three tries to get Spencer's attention as he continued to sing Old Macdonald—he was really into it. A loud bellow of "*Hey!*" made my 5 year old jump and turn around.

"What are you doing?" I asked accusingly.

Spencer was a bright five-year old and he gave a bright five year olds' answer: "I dunno."

I'm ashamed to say I overreacted like…well…like a five year old! I ranted, raved and fumed. "This whole thing is ridiculous. What a waste of time. I never should have agreed to do this. Wes, get your pole. Spencer, get your—look, you've even lost your bobber. Never mind, just stay away, I'll get it."

As I grabbed the pole, I continued to vent. "We will not be going fishing again anytime soon!"

About that that time, a funny thing happened. I went to yank the fishing pole out of the water and it got caught on something. I glared at Spencer, thinking that he had hooked the proverbial fresh water log. I yanked again and the same thing happened.

Suddenly, it dawned on me that my kid had *actually hooked a fish*! I started to yell to Spencer that he had one on the line. He was so caught up in the moment that all he could do was jump up and down and twirl himself around like a top.

A rush of adrenalin shot through my body as I continued to yell, "you got one buddy, you got one!" I was now up to my ankles, trying to maneuver the fish on the end of the line closer to the shore. New sneakers? Who cares about new sneakers at a time like this?

The fish jumped up out of the water and I thought I had hooked a blue marlin. It was huge, with a great big mouth. I was now a lunatic on the beach between reaming at Spencer that he hooked Moby Dick and telling Wes that I needed the net. After much yelling and screaming, between the three of us we finally landed a 7½-pound large mouth bass. *A beauty*!

I was so happy and excited that I couldn't control myself. I was dancing with the kids and high-fiving like you wouldn't believe. We started doing chest bumps right on the beach and I'm embarrassed to say that I almost severely injured Spencer. I ran into him from about 5 yards away and delivered a chest bump that knocked him right on his behind. Little did I realize that I had knocked the wind out of him, until I picked him up and started dancing with him. Only then I heard his gasps, "Dad.....I.....ccccan't bbrrreathe!"

Once I saw that Spencer was okay, I turned towards Wes, not wanting to leave him out of the celebration. I turned and put my arms out for a hug. Somehow, I don't think he was too receptive after seeing what happened to his younger brother as his eyes bulged out and he screamed, "No, get away!"

We finally got things calmed down and headed to the car. I had brought along a small instamatic camera (Just in case we caught a fish). A young woman riding her bike stopped and took our picture.

I decided on the way home that we were going to go to Friendly's Ice Cream and the kids could have anything they wanted. As we headed there, I had the tunes cranking and I was feeling great about what had just happened. Actually, there are no words to describe how I was feeling. It was just surreal.

Then I heard the boys arguing in the back seat and Spencer telling Wes to be quiet. I turned down the music and asked what was going on. "Nothing!" came the dual reply from the back seat.

"Hey guys, you know we don't have any secrets from each other....what's going on?" Spencer, who always holds my feet to the fire, shouted back, "Hey Dad, you didn't want to be here today, did you?"

All the euphoria I was feeling after catching the fish and celebrating it with my sons was sucked out all at once by my son's question to me.

There is an indescribable feeling that comes over you when your children suddenly put you on the spot—especially when you know that *you were wrong*. I stammered, stuttered and stumbled over my words then said quietly, "You're right, pal, I did say that and I truly shouldn't have. I'm always talking about..."

Spencer cut me off and said, "That's OK dad, but I have another question for you."

I thought, oh boy, here it comes.

Spencer said simply, "Hey Dad, do you want to be here now?" To say that I was overcome with emotion would be an understatement, to say the least. A lump formed in my throat and I began to swallow hard. In an instant, I pulled my car over to the side of the road, and quickly hopped out. I have never in my life raised my hand or even spanked my kids but when I yanked open the back door to the car, they looked like the poor fish we had caught, mouths agape.

I erased their fears by jumping on them and telling them with tears in my eyes, "Guys, there's not another place in the world that I would rather be then here today with you both!"

The father of one of my good friends was famous for the phrase, "Someday I'm gonna' ..." Someday he was gonna' go to Disney World, someday he was gonna' take the family white water rafting, someday he was gonna' go see the Red Sox and Yankees in the Bronx. Someday he was gonna' but someday never came for him. He died of a heart attack at the age of 42, leaving a wife and 3 small children.

I took our "trophy" snap shot and had it enlarged. It's a wonderful picture that I have from that memorable day of July 17th. It has a sentence written underneath in bold lettering that simply states: *Always make the time in life for things that are important.*

Take it from a "former" workaholic: don't put off the hugs, don't put off saying "I love you" everyday, *and don't put off the things that are important.* Work will always be there and if you leave, someone will be right behind you to replace you. But no one can replace you in your children's lives.

Do you want to know how special our children are? Go in at night and look at them while they're sleeping. Then you will know why we were put on this earth. There is a famous sneaker company who has the perfect slogan, one that I love.

In the game of life, the most important game we will ever play—don't ever put things off—*just do it*!

Never A Dull Moment

in the Household

Because of my travel schedule, I am not your typical 9 to 5 dad. Time with my children is so special. I am an early riser—typically around 6:15 a.m. I get up, go downstairs, make the coffee and get juice ready for my 7-year old daughter who now has a great affinity for ESPN's SportsCenter.

Like clockwork, she typically arrives on my lap at 6:55 a.m. and I hand her a juice and a vitamin to get ready for the upcoming sports highlights. One morning recently, my daughter didn't arrive for the morning's normal rendition of sports. She was almost a half hour late! Naturally, the "protective" (and nosy) father in me kicked in, and I went to the top of the stairs to find my little princess huddled over the toilet.

When I asked her what she was doing, she started to well up and explain that while she wanted to surprise me by getting dressed and ready for school she had accidentally dropped her toothbrush in the toilet. *Note*: My daughter can get anything she wants from me by curling her lip and making her eyes water. Yeah, I'm a sucker.

Naturally, Super Daddy would save the day by going to get a pair of pliers and fishing the toothbrush out of the toilet. After dropping it in the wastebasket, I noticed my little girl fast-walk into the master bedroom, coming out with *my* toothbrush in her hand.

"Jessie, honey, what on earth are you doing with daddy's toothbrush?" I exclaimed.

To which my 7-year old put her hand on her hip and looked at me like she was 20 years old, then said: "Daddy, we better throw this one away also—it fell in the toilet 2 day's ago!"

Laughter is definitely contagious. It's good for the mind, and great for the soul. I hope you get as much out of reading this story as I do telling it. *Priceless!*

 Family

A man and woman had been married for just about 6 years. They had a little 4-year old boy who was the apple of their eye. The man's father-in-law was into his late 80's and could no longer live by himself. The old man, they decided would come to live with them.

The old man's step faltered, his eyesight was failing and he was very unsteady on his feet. Every evening the family ate together at the table but the elderly man's shaky hands and eyesight made it difficult. He dropped food constantly, spilled his drink onto the floor and dropped dishes all the time.

The couple tried to ignore it but the Grandfather was making it quite difficult. After many weeks of this the husband became irritated with the mess and laid into his wife about her father. "We have to do something about your dad. He eats like a pig and I'm sick and tired of cleaning up after him" he yelled one night. Neither one of them wanted to put the elderly man in a nursing home so they decided that they would set a small table in the corner where he could sit by himself. There, the Grandfather sat and ate alone while the husband, wife and son enjoyed their dinner. Sometimes, the little boy would notice a tear in his Grandfather's eye but the husband and wife noticed nothing.

Because he broke so many dishes the couple served the Grandfather's meals in a plastic bowl. The little boy watched all of this and said nothing. One evening, the husband noticed his son playing with a bunch of plastic pieces on the floor. He asked his son what he was making. The boy cheerfully responded, "Oh, I'm making a little bowl for you and mommy to eat your food in when I grow up."

The words so struck the husband that he felt a giant lump form in his throat. He looked at his wife and saw tears coming down her cheeks. Neither of them said a word. That evening, the husband took his father-in-law, put his arm around him and slowly lead him back to the table.

For the remainder of the Grandfather's days he ate all of his meals with the family. And for some reason, the husband and wife no longer cared if a fork was dropped and anything was spilled.

The most important thing in life? *Family*.

Never Take Yourself Too Seriously

I had just finished a corporate speaking engagement in Orlando, Florida several years ago and was returning to the airport. After the arduous task of checking in and going through security, I found comfort at the airport terminal with a cup of coffee and my USA Today.

While reading, I got the strange sensation that someone was watching me. I dropped my paper and several times tried to figure out who the culprit was that was invading my space. Suddenly, I made eye contact with a person about 30 feet across the terminal—a lovely young woman in her late 70's/early 80's.

So, after several awkward seconds I returned her smile and went back to reading my newspaper. The next thing I knew, the woman was standing over me with an even bigger smile on her face. She bent down over me and spoke softly in my ear. "I just wanted to tell you that my husband and I thoroughly enjoy listening to you." I looked around and with a half-doubting smile, said *"me?"* I was always taught that flattery would get you everywhere!

Now ladies and gentleman, I was in my 2nd year at ESPN Radio and I would be lying if I said that my ego wasn't kicking in. 1 changed to my "radio voice" which was half Wayne Soares and half Elvis. The woman went on and on. "We just love your voice and the way that you come across and....." I interrupted the woman and asked her what her name was. She replied, "Mary." I said, "Well, Mary, you have a safe trip and a wonderful day and thank you for the kind words." She said, "Oh, I *will* have a great day because when I get home, I'm going to tell my husband that I met the *great* Bryant Gumbel!"

And do you know that for the next 5 minutes I could not convince that woman that I wasn't Bryant Gumbel. She finally said nicely, "I guess that you just don't want anyone to know who you are" and turned around ever so happily and walked away.

If I had a huge ego, I would have been offended for the woman mistaking me for someone else. It was a nice compliment to be mistaken for Bryant Gumbel. He's a consummate professional that has enjoyed an extraordinary career in broadcasting. I wish I had his money!

The above is proof that we should *never* take ourselves too serious. In life, in sports, at work and around family and friends

The Art of Humility

Muhammad Ali has always been one of my great idols. Not only for the stand he took back in the 1960's when he refused to go to Vietnam and stood against the United States government, but for his wonderful personality, charm and the way that he handles himself around the old and the young. Ali definitely has God-given charisma and a huge presence.

Back in the early 1970's, he was getting ready for an upcoming title bout with his archrival and hated opponent, Joe Frazier. The two men really didn't care for each other and Ali's endless taunts and instigation didn't help.

One day while he was training in his gym, Ali was approached by a member of his entourage who wondered if it would be possible for Ali to make a visit to his father in a nursing home in the next town.

Ali was always ready to take things to the next level and said that he would not only spend time with the old gentleman, but with the entire nursing home. The man was delighted and thanked Ali profusely. True to his word the day arrived when Ali was to visit the nursing home. At precisely 9 a.m., Ali's giant tour bus pulled into the nursing home parking lot. Sixty-five people got out of the bus and headed for the entrance.

Ali made himself at home at the reception desk by amusing the nurses and staff with jokes and card tricks before being lead up to the elderly man's room. When he walked through the door; the old man couldn't believe his eyes and a huge smile came across his face as he sat there in disbelief. Ali sat down, did several magic tricks with the man and stayed with him for about a half hour bringing him much needed laughter before a member of his entourage said that it was time to go.

In typical fashion, Ali leaned over the man, lifted his hat and kissed him on the forehead, whispering, "you better get better pop, or I'm gonna' come back and whip you." The warmth and kindness Ali showed absolutely made the old man's day. After visiting everyone throughout the nursing home, Ali was being lead out of the building by two nurses when he passed the TV room and went back to stare in. Sitting all alone by himself in a wheelchair was an elderly gentleman with a shawl draped over his legs fast asleep.

Ali inquired as to who the man was, and was told that his name was Mr. Jones and that he was a former semi-pro boxer. The nurse also relayed that Mr. Jones had dementia and was losing his eyesight. "It won't make a difference if he can see you or not," she said. To which Ali replied, "It will to me. Now will you please get me a chair and put it in front of this man."

Sitting down in front of the man, Ali reached out and shook his leg gently. The man's head bobbed up for a second, then went right back down. This time, Ali shook his leg a little firmer, but still gently. Suddenly the old man's eyes opened and his mouth dropped. He started to shake violently.

Ali asked the man "Do you know who I am?" The man replied, "You da' Champ.... You da' Champ." Then he proceeded to break down and sob uncontrollably. Ali took out his handkerchief and wiped the old man's tears, assuring him that everything would be OK. The old man began telling Ali that he was so sorry for crying but that his whole life he had wanted to meet him. "I've waited so long, champ—so long and now the day has come. I have only one living relative and that's my daughter," he said. "She is my greatest treasure but meeting you today—outside of the birth of my daughter—is the greatest thing that has ever happened to me in my life."

Ali was completely floored and thanked the man for sharing that with him. But he wanted to ask him something before he left. Taking the man's hand and holding it in his, Ali asked the man the simple question. "Hey pop, tell me before I leave, what's my name?" And the old man looked him right in the eye, not missing a beat and exclaimed in all seriousness, "you—you're Joe Louis—the Heavyweight Champion of the World!"

Upon hearing that, all of Ali's entourage began to scream and curse at the man, which brought Ali into a state of blind fury. He yelled at everyone to get out of the room and wait across the hall in the activities room. After helping the man regain his composure and fix his glasses and shawl, he looked directly at the nurse and told her not to move this man until he returned. Then Ali tore across the hall to the room where his entourage nervously waited.

Upon entering, Ali slammed the door with such force that two pictures fell and broke to the floor. He let his presence sink in for about 10 seconds then spoke.

"Did you hear what that man said?" he asked. He repeated himself again and no one said anything. Finally he screamed, *"Did you hear what that man said?"* A member of his entourage spoke up and said, "yeah, that old goat, he called you Joe Louis. Man, you're Ali! The greatest of all time...."

Ali shook his head sadly, pointed to his heart and said again, "did you hear what that man said?" Nobody dared to answer. Ali said, "that man told me that outside of the birth of his most precious possession, his beloved daughter, that meeting *me* is the greatest thing that has ever happened to him in his life. Don't you get it?" Again, no one could answer.

Then Ali said, "I want everyone in this room to listen and listen good. For the rest of the time that we spend in this nursing home today, you remember one thing: *My name is Joe Louis.*"

And that, ladies and gentlemen is what is called humility. No matter how good we think we are, we should always be *humble*.

Super Dad

I remember when my two boys were seven and nine: I loved them dearly, and didn't hesitate to correct them with "tough love." However, I found when my daughter came along that there is something different about a baby girl, especially mine! She was born a *Princess* and knew it instantly. She got her tiny hands around my heart that first day and has never let go. She has been turning me into a large marshmallow ever since.

A few years ago, when she was three, I came home only to be greeted by the cries and screams of my little girl. She apparently had somehow pinched her finger in a cabinet drawer while Mommy had stepped downstairs to check on the laundry.

There are many things that can bring a father to his knees when it comes to his children, and certainly one of them is seeing his daughter in tears. Rushing into the living room, I morphed into Super Dad, looking around for a telephone booth, ready to change into suit and cape. I'm always at the ready to give hugs and to kiss the 'boo-boos' away. The boys often wonder why their father, who tells them all the time to "act like a man" and "shake it off," turns into Florence Nightingale when his little girl is crying.

Tossing my briefcase aside, I got down on all fours and took my daughter's hand in mine. I quickly kissed the index finger that she was holding up in the air. This had always been a sure cure in similar situations. Now I watched for the return of her normally sunny smile but this was not to be—not this time! Instead, she quickly snatched her hand away from me and started to cry and scream even louder than before.

"Honey," I protested, "Daddy was only trying to make it better." She drew herself up—suddenly a regal presence worthy of the Queen Mother addressing a boorish commoner. My little Princess, now full of royal indignation, said, "Daddy—you just kissed my boogie!"

Tell me, have you ever been there?

What Would *You* Do?

Several years ago, when I first got into motivational speaking I met an extraordinary young man named Tommy Phillips. Tommy was a junior in high school and possessed some truly wonderful characteristics. He was polite, courteous, had an unbelievable personality, a strong leader (captain of his football and baseball teams), great team player—he was a kid that after you had a conversation with him you went, "WOW, that kid is going places." In essence, he was a joy to have around and you knew that this young man was blessed with unique skills.

With all that he had going for him, Tommy made a tragic mistake that ended up costing him his life. At an after hours prom party, he drank way too much, got into his car and proceeded to drive head first into a telephone pole. The car exploded on impact and he was killed instantly.

Outside of the passing of my grandparents, Tommy's wake and funeral were the worst events that I ever had to go through. Everyone that attended the wake put a red rose into Tommy's casket. After watching this for over two hours I became so angry that I wanted to take every single one of those red roses, rip them to shreds and throw them out the window. You ask why would I do such a thing?

Because everyone of those so called "student-athletes" and "student leaders" that were putting roses in Tommy's casket were the same people that were at the party with him and allowed him to get in his car and drive himself into a telephone pole. If someone had taken the time to talk to him and showed just a tiny bit of leadership, Tommy would probably be with us today.

But nobody cared and nobody took the time.

I never make it a habit to preach to young kids or young men and women. But *please* take it from Wayne Anthony Soares, a father himself. When you are put into a difficult situation and you might not think of it as a life-threatening one at the time, *please* think of all of your options and make a good decision. Your parents won't be there, your coaches won't be. No one will be there except for *you*.

Young people have so much ahead of them and when you make a careless decision that costs you your life, you can *never* come back when that page is turned.

And if you're a parent that is reading this, remember this: Tommy Phillips did not call home that fateful evening because he had an argument with his father and didn't want to talk to him. Like I tell my kids, I would much rather get a phone call at 2 a.m. to come and pick you up at the police station than a phone call from the hospital morgue.

Take Time to Make a Difference

This is a story that I tell often whenever I speak. It is very powerful and exemplifies what true friendship is all about. There was a young boy named Rob who was in Junior High School in the 7th grade.

Rob's dad was in the military, so Rob was never able to get adjusted to one place for a particular amount of time. Rob was an extremely quiet young boy, had thick glasses, a bit of acne and was a little uncoordinated. Because of his features, this made him an easy target for bullies.

Rob dreaded the start of the new school year and once again felt uncomfortable in his new surroundings. After a week, he still didn't have any friends, and the taunts and vicious remarks from the school bullies were starting to wear on him. After a month, it became almost unbearable. Rob actually had to walk in the middle of the school hallway or the bullies would push him into the lockers.

One Friday afternoon, 7th grader Tom Sullivan was on his way home from football practice. Tom was easily the most popular kid at the Junior High School. All the girls loved him and would giggle when he would walk by, and all the boys held him in awe because of his athletic ability. He was, by nature, a good kid that was liked by his teachers and peers.

He was thinking about the pizza party he was going to have at his house that evening with some of his teammates, when he noticed someone coming at him about 100 yards away.

It was a tall, thin kid with a huge number of books under both arms. The kid seemed to be struggling not to drop any. "Why is this kid carrying all those books home on a Friday afternoon—must be pretty smart!" Tom thought to himself. Suddenly, out of nowhere came three of the school bullies. Tom watched the bullies race at Rob full force while Rob tried to shield himself from the oncoming blows.

They hit him with such force that Rob's books and glasses went flying and he crashed to the ground, hitting his head on the pavement. Upon seeing this, Tom Sullivan froze in his tracks for about 5 seconds, then—filled with rage—proceeded to chase after the bullies. He was screaming at the top of his lungs when they ran around the corner and out of sight.

Stopping in front of Rob with his chest heaving, he bent down and helped the stunned boy who was trying to struggle to his feet. When their eyes met, Tom was taken back at the look of pure hurt that he saw on Rob's face. Never in his life had he seen a look of such pain. "Hey, those guys are just idiots, ya' know.......you OK?" he offered, trying to make conversation. "I…I…I just need to get home. Leave me alone....I'll be alright....just leave me alone," countered Rob.

"I'm Tom Sullivan," he said, sticking out his hand. "You're new in school aren't you?"

"I'm Rob Smith" Rob answered barely above a whisper. For the next 10 minutes, Tom tried to get Rob to come to his house and join in that night's pizza party. Rob was adamant and kept saying, "I really need to get home." Tom—equally as stubborn—refused to let Rob leave until he at least came and met his parents. Finally, Rob reluctantly agreed.

When he came into the Sullivan home, Rob could not believe it. For the first time in many, many years, he felt relaxed and comfortable. Tom's parents were kind and warm, and made Rob feel right at home. Tom's pals were cool too, asking him about the different places he had been and what his favorite sports teams were. They even said that with his height, he should think about trying out for the football team!

From that day forward, Rob & Tom were inseparable. They were like brothers and did everything together for the next 5 years. One day, when Tom was a high school senior, he walked through the cafeteria doors and stopped dead in his tracks—he couldn't believe what he saw. Sitting at a huge table in the cafeteria, surrounded by pretty girls and guys, was Rob. He had grown into a handsome young man. Gone were the dark, thick glasses (replaced by contacts), his acne had disappeared and not only was he one of the best athletes in the school but he was Valedictorian of his graduating class. The bullies at the school now held *him* in awe.

Tom couldn't have been happier for his friend. He felt a warmth come over him that he had never experienced before. He truly was happy for Rob and all that he achieved. When they were alone at the table, Rob confided to Tom that he was really nervous about having to give a speech the following week at graduation. Tom assured him that he would do just fine. "Take a deep breath and just let it go," he told his pal.

The evening of graduation, the auditorium was jammed packed with over 1,000 people. Rob sat nervously in his seat and made eye contact with Tom, who gave him the thumbs up sign. When his name was called, Rob strode to the podium like a true professional. Putting his notes on the podium, he took a deep breath and began to read.

"There are many things in my life that I am thankful for. I have had wonderful parents, great teachers and great coaches. But the one thing that I will be forever grateful for is the action of my best friend." He looked down and smiled at his best friend Tom.

Rob began to tell the story of the first day that he met Rob and how he was bringing all of his books home that Friday after school because he didn't want his mother to have to clean out his locker on Monday. Tom was confused. "Clean out his locker?" he thought.

Rob stunned everyone in the crowd when he confided that he was bringing all of his books home that day because he was going to go home and commit suicide. For years and years, he had endured physical and verbal abuse at the hands of some mean and vicious kids and he had finally had enough.

"It was because of the brave actions of my best friend Tom Sullivan that I stand before you today. Tom took the time with someone he didn't know and saved me from doing the unthinkable. He is the bravest person and the best friend that anyone could ever have."

One person can make a difference in many lives. Look at Martin Luther King, John F. Kennedy and Thomas Edison. They were just one person and they made a huge difference. What would you do in that situation?

The True Art of Teamwork

Several years ago at the National Special Olympics in Seattle, WA, one of the most fantastic and memorable events took place in a stadium of 15,000 spectators. Everyone watched as 10 Special Olympians lined up to compete in the 100-yard dash. The judge walked over to the starting line, raised his starter's gun and fired. All of the 11-year-old participants started running as fast as they possibly could. 10 yards… 20 yards. Right around the 30-yard mark, a little boy was running so fast that he completely lost his balance and spun right out of control, smashing to the pavement.

The spectators gasped in horror as the other nine participants kept right on running. The boy was now crying on his back and had a big gash on his chin and a scrape on his leg from hitting the pavement. Then suddenly, upon hearing the boy's cries—which had now grown into a loud wail—the other nine Olympians stopped and froze for about five seconds. Slowly, they all began to walk back to the boy and formed a protective circle around him.

One little girl who had Down Syndrome knelt beside the boy and urged him to get up saying, "we're going to finish this race together." They all struggled to pull the boy to his feet and turned him around. Then the most remarkable thing happened. All of the kids linked arms and proceeded to walk slowly toward the finish line. Step by step.

And what you heard in that stadium of 15,000 people was one clap turned into two claps and five hundred turned into a thousand and pretty soon all of the people in the stadium were standing, cheering and shouting encouragement to the kids as all ten of them crossed the finish line at the exact same time.

What matters most in our life is not winning for yourself—it is helping others win too. It is using the talents and abilities that you have been given to make a positive impact in someone else's life every day.

Sam Jacobs

A young boy about 12 years old walked into a pharmacy one day and proceeded to go over to the phone and put a couple of quarters in. He dialed a number and an elderly woman answered on the other end. The boy began, "Ma'am, my name is Sam Jacobs and I'd like to cut your lawn for $5."

Obviously flustered, the woman said somewhat sharply, "I *already* have someone that does that for me and I'm happy with him. Now I'm already late to an appointment so.. ...." The young boy cut her off and exclaimed, "but Ma'am, I will not only cut your grass for $5 but I will also take out all of your trash once a week for the same price."

The woman was now annoyed and wanted to end this discussion. She said, "I have someone that cuts my lawn and takes out my trash, now if you'll excuse me I....." Once again the boy politely interrupted and said, "Ma'am, I have the deal of the century for you! Not only will I cut your grass, take out your trash, but I will go to the grocery store for you during the week as well—*all for the price of $5.* Now you can't beat that, can you?"

This time, the woman's voice became very motherly as she talked to the young boy. "Son," she said, "as I've tried to explain to you, I already have someone that cuts my lawn and takes out my trash *and* I have someone that does all of my shopping too. He is a very kind, polite and courteous young man just like you. I am very happy with what he does for me and love him like a son."

The boy thanked the woman and apologized for making her late to her scheduled appointment and hung up the phone. As he turned around, the owner of the store was standing in front of him—an elderly gentleman with green pants and a flannel shirt.

"That was quite a job you did there on the phone with that lady, young fella," exclaimed the man. The boy thanked him and started to walk away. The storeowner said, "You know, I could use someone like you around here. You have such a great personality and you're a real people person."

The boy was quite flattered but said that he could not accept a position at the store. The old man wondered why. After dropping his head and pausing for about 5 seconds the boy looked up and said, "Sir, my name isn't really Sam Jacobs." The old man gave the boy a puzzled look. "Sir, I am the boy that cuts that woman's lawn, takes out her trash and does all of her shopping for her—*I just wanted to see what type of job she thought I was doing.*"

Everything you do in life, everything you attempt, do it with *pride*—take pride in who you are and your accomplishments.

Being Judgmental:
Things Aren't Always
The Way They Appear

The little girl was 6 years old when she first began to ask questions about her mother's hands. Both were burned and terribly disfigured. In her typical way, the mother brushed her daughter's questions aside and said that she had been careless around the stove several years ago and since she was not paying attention, her hands were badly burned.

This seemed to satisfy the daughter but she took it upon herself to hide her mother's hands from everyone. When the little girl turned eight years old, she had become infatuated with covering her mother's hands. Everyday after school, she would race home and run upstairs to take a pair of white gloves from her mother's dresser. She would then run downstairs and tell the mother to put them on because she had friends coming over. The mother would never say a word and took the gloves and put them on, going about her household chores.

This same pattern went on after school and before any big event that the girl was involved with or would attend. In each instance, the mother took the gloves without saying a word and put them over her disfigured hands.

When the girl's high school prom night came, she was never concerned about her dress, her date or what type of an evening she was going to have. All she cared about was making sure that her mother put on her white gloves when her date came to pick her up. The same routine continued throughout the girl's college years—whenever she brought home a friend, the mother had to put on her white gloves, never saying a word.

Several years later, the young girl had turned into a beautiful woman and was to be married. She looked like a princess in her beautiful gown and with her hair all done up. It was the biggest day of her life and all she would worry about was whether or not her mother remembered to bring her white gloves with her. The mother assured her that she hadn't forgotten, holding up her gloved hands.

The mother went on to enjoy a wonderful life. Her daughter lived nearby and had presented her with a beautiful granddaughter a few years before. Her daughter had been the apple of her eye and her most treasured possession her whole life, and she was very thankful.

Well into her eighties, the woman finally passed away of natural causes. As the daughter, her husband and father went to the funeral home to make arrangements, they went to view the woman's body. Upon seeing her mother in a casket, the daughter proceeded to take out a white pair of gloves from her purse. As she walked towards the casket ready to put them on her mother's hands, the father stopped her and spoke. "Your mother never wanted me to share this with you but now that she is gone I think I will."

The girl looked at her father, feeling somewhat bewildered. The father began, "When you were first born; I used to travel a great deal and was gone for long periods of time. Because of that, your mother had to wear many hats. One evening during the holidays when I wasn't home, your mother awoke to the smell of smoke. Jumping out of bed and opening the bedroom door, she was blinded by the black smoke that filled the hallway. Getting on her hands and knees, she crawled into your room to find that a Christmas light had caught fire on the curtain right next to your crib. Flames were inside your crib and you were seconds from being severely burned. Your mother rushed in and immediately started to whack the flames with her hands. She then snatched you out of the crib and brought you to safety outside the house."

The daughter felt so ashamed that she had been embarrassed by her mother's deformity and asked her father why she never said anything. "Because your mother was too proud of you and didn't want you to know," replied the father.

Sometimes we see people that are different and don't act or look the way we want them to. *Never* judge someone, because you have no idea as to what they might be experiencing or going through.

The Power of Being Positive

I grew up without a father in my life. Because my mom worked hard being a single parent, I spent a great deal of time with my grandmother. I worshiped the ground that she walked on and even named my daughter after her as a loving tribute. To this day, she remains the greatest person I have ever met in my life. She is no longer with us but I think of her and the lessons that she taught me every day.

One day over breakfast, she asked me if I would like to attend a major league baseball autograph signing in downtown Boston. There was one player on the Boston Red Sox that I completely idolized. I wanted to throw like him, I wanted to bat like him -- I even ran in from the field like he would. His pictures covered the walls of this 12-year olds' room.

Naturally, I was overjoyed when Gram said that she would take me to meet my idol. I could barely sleep the night before and awakened before the birds that Saturday morning. I woofed down my breakfast and headed to the car, complete with baseball cap and glove.

Now I mentioned earlier that my Grandmother was the greatest person I have ever known, but there was one thing that she wasn't particularly good at and that was directions. She was absolutely *horrendous* at directions!

We took off from our house in Falmouth on Cape Cod, MA and headed towards Boston. The trip typically takes anywhere from an hour and fifteen minutes to an hour and a half (we ended up driving around New Hampshire completely lost!).

I begged my Grandmother to please take me to the hotel where the autograph signing was being held, pleading with her as we backtracked to Boston. She finally said yes and we pulled into the parking garage underneath the hotel. I jumped out of the car and we headed into the hotel. I raced up to the front desk and was heartbroken to learn that my idol had left almost an hour ago.

To say that I was crushed was the understatement of the year. I turned around and was going to have the biggest temper tantrum of the year when the young front desk clerk told me that my idol might just be in the hotel restaurant. "Just go down the hallway, take a left and quick right and you will see the restaurant right in front of you," she said.

Looking like the roadrunner on Bugs Bunny, I raced to the restaurant blazing a trail of fire behind me. Running to the front of the restaurant, I stopped dead in my tracks when I looked inside. There, sitting all by himself was none other than my idol! I was star struck, happy—my euphoria was uncontrollable! No one else was in the restaurant except a waitress and she had *no clue* as to who was sitting there.

I absolutely floated over on a cloud, ladies and gentleman. Here was a real chance to do some male bonding with my favorite, all-time baseball player—just him and me. I approached his table and was petrified. I turned around to see my grandmother blowing me kisses, smiling and clutching her pocketbook and this made me feel just a little more secure. The aforementioned was about the size of a mailman's sack and had everything that you could possibly imagine inside of it. It didn't matter where we were, if I said that my shirt was wrinkled, Gram would say, "don't worry dear, I have an iron right here" and pull one from her bag (this also worked with wiffle ball bats and oars).

In any event, I stood in front of my idol and had no clue what to say when suddenly I blurted out, "Sir, my name is Wayne Soares and I am a *huge* fan of yours and I came here today with my Grandmother to get your autograph because we got lost and missed the one that started earlier and man, I would just *love* to get your autograph." My idol didn't even look at me and kept eating his lunch.

Now I had thought that because he had spent all day signing hundreds of autographs that perhaps he was a bit tired of the autograph scene. Maybe I can get some baseball advice from my idol! I'll get some advice first-hand and go back to the boys in the neighborhood and I'll *really* be the big cheese.

So being a big baseball fan, I asked my idol a typical baseball-fan-question: "what's the best way to hit a curveball?" Easy question, right? I was dreaming of the answer that I would get and what I would tell the kids back in my Falmouth Heights neighborhood when I was jolted out of my dream. When I asked my baseball idol my "what's the best way to hit a curveball" question, he responded with an angry, "*with a bat, kid!*" and went back to eating his lunch.

There are no words to describe how his words knifed through me and how much they stung. It was like someone came up in front of me and hit me as hard as they could. I was stunned and numb as I walked away. This person had the chance to make an impact on a young kid and threw the chance away. This man had the opportunity to send a 12-year old kid off with a memorable experience—he did but in the wrong way.

He could have given me 30 seconds out of his day to *make my day*. The power of what we say to others is immense. The way we talk to our parents, the way parents talk to their kids, the way we talk to each other. You can make a positive impact in someone else's life by taking 5 or 10 seconds to say something nice to them. When you look at it realistically, it truly is quite easy.

Be that person that will make a *positive impact* in someone's life—at work, on the bus, at school or wherever. Remember, we are ***all*** role models.

3 Seconds

When my youngest son was eight years old, he decided that he wanted to try out for youth basketball. It was a good idea and I volunteered to coach his team. The kids were great and easy to coach.

My brand of basketball was entertaining for the kids and they seemed to enjoy it. We practiced high fives, cheering for your teammates, hustle, shaking hands after you lose, good sportsmanship and, of course, fundamentals.

One Saturday, we were set to play a team whose coach was a little bit "over the edge," if you know what I mean. His warm-up routine consisted of push-ups, wind sprints and sit-ups with him barking at the kids that they "better be ready to play." This guy had begun to get a reputation within the youth ranks as a loudmouth that yells at his players.

My son's pal Timmy played on the team, and during warm-ups he went over to say hello to his friend. While the kids were chatting, the coach barked to Timmy, "get over here—we don't talk to the other team before the game." I thought, "This guy can't be for real."

Timmy's dad was in attendance that day and he had always struck me as the kind of guy who was living his sports career through his kid. In any event, we started the game and jumped out to a 10-2 lead. Timmy came down the court and was whistled for three seconds by the young high school student referee. The coach immediately jumped off the bench, looked at Timmy and screamed "three seconds Timmy! Let's go, wake up!"

The next time down the floor, Timmy did the exact same thing and got whistled for another three second violation. This put the coach into a rage as he called Timmy over and berated him in front of the bench. "You better get your head in the game, son, or you'll be sitting next to me," he yelled.

Timmy's dad now joined in and yelled for him to *"focus... focus!"* Did I mention that these were eight-year-old kids?

Both teams exchanged baskets the next couple of times down the floor. Timmy was petrified to touch the ball. It seemed like the father and coach were all over this kid, yelling at him to *"get in the game."* He was disoriented and confused and got whistled for three seconds again. This brought the coach off of the bench. Eyes blazing, he met Timmy at half court, grabbed him by his shirt and continued to yell and embarrass him as he physically dragged him to the bench.

Timmy's dad had made his way down to the bench. I thought, "great—he is going to set this coach straight." Instead, he started yelling at his son from behind as the coach continued his abusive behavior! Calling the referee over, I said to him: "Either you do something about this, or I will." The high school student had a tremendous amount of courage and guts because he threatened the coach with an ejection and told the father to get away from the bench immediately—what a guy!

After the game, Timmy was still sitting on the bench when I went over to tell him that he played a good game and to keep his head up. But instead, he kept his head down and I could see little drops of tears start to hit the gymnasium floor. "Hey pal, you have to keep your head up and just get ready for the next game," I said. Timmy looked up at me with huge, sad eyes and said something that I will never forget. "Mr. Soares, I don't even know what 'three seconds' means."

We need to teach our kids the fundamentals of sports, how to play the game properly, and how to lose with grace and dignity. Our society is so bent on winning, winning, winning, so consequently when kids lose, they don't know how to handle it and think that they are failures.

Teach your child how to lose. It will only help them down the road.

How Much Fun
Did You Have Playing?

Everybody should grow up in a neighborhood where you have
to make up different games. I used to love Kick The Can, Stickball,
Wiffle Ball, Bombardment, Hide and Seek, Flashlight Tag—these
were the *best* and we played them all the time!

I used to get up and just go play for the whole day when I was
a kid. And do you know the first thing my grandmother asked me
when I came through the door? It wasn't "Did you win?" It wasn't
"How many hits or goals did you get?" It was just a simple question:
"Did you have fun?" So simple, yet to the point: "Did you have fun?"

Many of the moms and dads of today sit and scream at the
umpire or referee because they are frustrated themselves. They think
it's someone else's fault because their kid didn't do well. The kid, in
turn, finds so many excuses in defeat or with a poor performance.

Whenever you make excuses after a defeat or a poor
performance, you are having a guilty conscience because you weren't
prepared and you didn't give 110%.

We continue to lose sight of the joy and fun of sports. Youth sports is supposed to be fun and enjoyable! If you're not loving the sport that you play—if you don't enjoy practicing—then do yourself a favor and find something that you *can* enjoy.

When the game is over, you should be happy at the effort and what you contributed.

YES I CAN - A Final, Personal Note

I mentioned that I grew up without a father in my life. I was very active in sports, and was fortunate enough to be shuttled back and forth to practices by my Grandfather, Grandmother and my Mother. They were my biggest fans and rarely missed one of my games in baseball and basketball. Gramp even sent me to Ted Williams' Camp four years in a row. What a thrill! Sports was my life.

Growing up with no father, there were some painful memories as well. I remember being devastated after one of the adult local yokels told me that I would never amount to anything in life "because I didn't have a father." I remember the kids in elementary and middle school saying mean and vicious things to me on Father's Day and at father & son events.

In Junior High School, I was horrified to sit at my desk one day and look down to see these words written; "I'm Wayne Soares and I don't have:

A.) A Father   B.) A Dad or C.) All of The Above"

Boy, did that sting for weeks. I have learned through the experience of being a father myself that *anyone* can be a father, but it takes a *very* special person to be a *dad*.

Perhaps you might have had the same experience as me. If so, I want to tell you a story about never giving up. There was a young boy in Junior High School that loved playing basketball. Everywhere he went, he carried a basketball and was always playing. The young boy decided that he would try out for his Junior High's team. For five days he hustled, dove on the floor and gave 110%. On the final day of tryouts, the boy was called into the coach's office.

For five minutes the coach went on about what a great team player the boy was and how he admired his hustle, finally adding, "Son, in my 15 years of coaching, you have the best attitude I've ever seen but I'm gonna' have to cut you because you don't have enough talent to make this team." Upon hearing those words, all of the air was completely sucked out of the boy. He felt sick to his stomach. Seeing this, the coach offered to make the boy Manager of the team. He could sit on the bench, dress up in a sport coat and tie, and even travel with the team to away games.

The boy politely declined. The coach then asked him what he was going to do. "I'm gonna' come back next year and make this team coach, because I'm gonna' work my tail off to get better." The coached thanked the boy, shook his hand and wished him good luck. As the boy walked out of his office, the coach thought that he would never see the boy again.

After a whole year, tryouts for the Junior High team were to be held on a Monday. True to his word, the young boy showed up once again. He had kept his promise and worked tremendously hard to make himself into a better player. He had improved every single facet of his game. And another funny thing happened in the off-season—the boy had grown six whole inches!

He not only made the team, but he *started every game*. From there he went on to set the career scoring mark at his High School. He received a full scholarship to play collegiate basketball (he also won an NCAA Championship). And from there? He went on to win *six* NBA Championships with the Chicago Bulls. That young boy's name was Michael Jordan, who in the prime of his career was (and is to date) the greatest basketball player ever to put on a pair of sneakers in the NBA.

The greatest basketball player the world has ever seen was cut from his Junior High School team. If Michael Jordan gave up and put his head in the sand and said "I can't be successful and achieve because someone told me so," there would be no Air Jordans, no NBA championships and no scoring titles. MJ said *yes I can* and he believed in himself and his ability. You can have all of the talent and ability in the world, but if you don't have *persistence* and *determination* you will always stay in the same place.

When that person told me that I couldn't be successful because I didn't have a father, it motivated me so much. *Yes I can!* Some people like to be negative in general. They said I wouldn't work at ESPN because "everyone is trying to get in there." I spent *six* years on the airwaves and interviewed everyone from Roger Clemens to Annika Sorrenstam to my idol Chris Berman! People said I could never become a public speaker because it's too competitive. I speak to major corporations and schools all over the country! I've even made presentations at Harvard University and the University of Notre Dame, and, I have been the featured speaker at six college commencement ceremonies. Not bad for a guy that graduated from North Adams State College with a 2.3 GPA!

People were amazed when I told them that I was writing a book. *"You?"* they would say (every once in a while a blind squirrel finds a nut!). My point being that if you are determined and *really* put your mind to something, there isn't anything that you cannot achieve in your life.

From the time I was a youngster, people were telling me that I couldn't be successful. When someone tells you that remember these three important words: *Yes I can!*

About the Author

Wayne Soares is a successful motivational speaker, television host and stand-up comedian. A frequent guest at the Basketball Hall of Fame's "MVP in Character" series, his humorous style, energy and passion are a favorite with his audiences.

Wayne's appearances take him to the halls of the nation's most distinguished colleges (Harvard University, Williams College and the University of Notre Dame) and into some of the best schools in the country.

After spending 6 seasons on the airwaves at ESPN Radio as a broadcaster, Wayne left to pursue an acting and TV career in Hollywood. In 2006, he co-starred in a television pilot sports/comedy show for Fox Sports Net titled "Regular Joe's" which was filmed in Los Angeles, CA.

Wayne will begin filming and hosting his new TV show "The Everyday Fan" this fall at the Mohegan Sun Casino in CT. He devotes his charitable time to the Maine & Massachusetts Special Olympics and is the immensely proud father of three children: Wesley & Spencer and a little girl, Jessie.

Also Available From Summerland Publishing

Have you ever contemplated how to go about explaining the concept of integrity to a five year old? Don't you wish children would have a better understanding of the core values so often eluding them in today's society, *especially in the face of all of the unethical actions taking place in our capitol these days?* Bud Bottoms, an internationally acclaimed sculptor of ocean life, has written a book called *Kid Ethics* that responds to this void in a child's education. Summerland Publishing has now released *Kid Ethics 2*, a follow-up to the original *Kid Ethics*, both of which can make a major impact on the world.

While *Kid Ethics* is geared towards children ages 5-10, it can be enlightening for the whole family. Mr. Bottoms takes the letters of the alphabet and assigns an ethic to each. Things like honesty, justice and open-mindedness are explained with short stories to which everyone can relate. They are accompanied by the author's pleasant illustrations that can be colored in by the reader. A two-line poem then summarizes the ethic, making it easier to digest.

U.S.$12.95/Can. $17.95   ISBN: 0-9794863-1-9

Order from:
www.summerlandpublishing.com, www.barnesandnoble.com,
www.amazon.com or find it in your favorite bookstore!
Email SummerlandPubs@aol.com for more information.
Summerland Publishing, P. O. Box 493, Summerland, CA 93067